101 KNOCK KNOCK JOKES

VOLUME 3

THE HENNESSY KIDS

Featured Artwork by KATHERINE HENNESSY

Featured Artwork by SAMUEL HENNESSY

Featured Artwork by DANIEL HENNESSY

The Hennessy Entertainment
Company

101 Knock Knock Jokes Volume 3 / by The Hennessy Kids

ISBN 978-1-989621-10-3 (Print)

ISBN 978-1-989621-11-0 (E-book)

1. Wit and humor, Juvenile. 2. English wit and humor. I. The Hennessy Kids, author

The Hennessy Entertainment Company | HennessyEnt.com

To everybody who makes the fun stuff we enjoy.

1

NAME JOKES

Knock, knock.
  Who's there?
  John Cena.
  John Cena who?
  John Cena spider, now he's running scared.

Knock, knock.
  Who's there?
  Will.
  Will who?
  Will you let me in, its cold out here.

Knock, knock.
  Who's there?
  Barbie.
  Barbie who?
  Barbie Q Chicken is delicious.

Knock, knock.
> Who's there?
> Ken.
> Ken who?
> Ken you please open the door, Barbie?

Knock, knock.
> Who's there?
> Alda.
> Alda who?
> Alda good knock knock jokes are here, right?

Knock, knock.
> Who's there?
> Teresa.
> Teresa who?
> Teresa way to find out who I am, open the door.

Knock, knock.
> Who's there?
> Alli.
> Alli who?
> Alligator, that's who.

Knock, knock.
> Who's there?
> Hollis.
> Hollis who?
> Hollis not lost, we can still win.

Knock, knock.
>Who's there?
>Hugo.
>Hugo who?
>Hugo that way, and I'll go this way.

Knock, knock.
>Who's there?
>Isabelle.
>Isabelle who?
>Isabelle out of order? I had to knock.

Knock, knock.
>Who's there?
>Avery.
>Avery who?
>Avery time I come to your house we go through this.

Knock, knock.
>Who's there?
>Barry.
>Barry who?
>Barry the treasure in the backyard.

Knock, knock.
>Who's there?
>Ben.
>Ben who?
>Ben knocking so long my hand hurts.

Knock, knock.
    Who's there?
    Dewey.
    Dewey who.
    Dewey have to listen to all this knocking?

Knock, knock.
    Who's there?
    Doris.
    Doris who?
    Doris locked, that's why I'm knocking.

Knock, knock.
    Who's there?
    Douglas.
    Douglas who?
    Is douglas half empty or half full?

Knock, knock.
    Who's there?
    Felix.
    Felix who?
    Feel exhausted, let me in so I can rest.

Knock, knock.
    Who's there?
    Harmony.
    Harmony who?
    Harmony times do I have to tell you?

Knock, knock.
  Who's there?
  Harriet.
  Harriet who?
  Harriet up, and open the door.

Knock, knock.
  Who's there?
  Hayden.
  Hayden who?
  Do you wanna play Hayden seek?

Knock, knock.
  Who's there?
  Ivan.
  Ivan who?
  Ivan extremely sore hand from knocking.

Knock, knock.
  Who's there?
  Joe.
  Joe who?
  Joe King with you.

Knock, knock.
  Who's there?
  Ken.
  Ken who?
  Ken you tell me some good knock knock jokes?

Knock, knock.
　　Who's there?
　　Rhoda.
　　Rhoda who?
　　Row, row, Rhoda boat.

Knock, knock.
　　Who's there?
　　Shelby.
　　Shelby who?
　　Shelby comin' round the mountain when she comes.

Knock, knock.
　　Who's there?
　　Shirley.
　　Shirley who?
　　Shirley you must know me by now.

Knock, knock.
　　Who's there?
　　Stu.
　　Stu who?
　　Stu late to ask questions.

Knock, knock.
　　Who's there?
　　Theodore.
　　Thedore who?
　　Theodore is shut, please open it.

Knock, knock.
>Who's there?
>Candace.
>Candace who?
>Candace day get any better? No.

FEATURED ARTWORK #1

Knock, Knock. Who's there? Deluxe. Deluxe who? Deluxe Ness Monster.
(Artwork by Katherine Hennessy)

2

FOOD JOKES

Knock, knock.
   Who's there?
   Pecan!
   Pecan who?
   Pecan somebody your own size.

Knock, knock.
   Who's there?
   Hungry clock!
   Hungry clock who?
   Hungry clock who went back four seconds.

Knock, knock.
   Who's there?
   Closure.
   Closure who?
   Closure mouth while you're chewing.

Knock, knock.
    Who's there?
    Bean.
    Bean who?
    Bean a while since I last saw ya.

Knock, knock.
    Who's there?
    Egg.
    Egg who?
    Egg-cited to see me?

Knock, knock.
    Who's there?
    Four Eggs.
    Four Eggs who?
    Four Eggs sample.

Knock, knock.
    Who's there?
    Handsome.
    Handsome who?
    Handsome pizza to me please.

Knock, knock.
    Who's there?
    Ketchup.
    Ketchup who?
    Ketchup with me and I'll tell you.

Knock, knock.
> Who's there?
> Pasta.
> Pasta who?
> Pasta parmesan please.

Knock, knock.
> Who's there?
> Banana.
> Banana who?
> Banana split so it's just me.

Knock, knock.
> Who's there?
> Jalapeno.
> Jalapeno who?
> Am I getting jalapeno business?

Knock, knock.
> Who's there?
> Two 4's
> Two 4's who?
> No need to make lunch we already 8.

Knock, knock.
> Who's there?
> Pizza!
> Pizza who?
> Pete's a really great guy.

Knock, knock.
 Who's there?
 Omelette!
 Omelette who?
 Omelette smarter than I look.

Knock, knock.
 Who's there?
 Avocado!
 Avocado who?
 Avocado cold.

Knock, knock.
 Who's there?
 Cash.
 Cash who?
 Oh, no, you're sick, too.

Knock, knock.
 Who's there?
 Falafel.
 Falafel who?
 Falafel off my bike and hurt my knee.

Knock, knock.
 Who's there?
 Turnip.
 Turnip who?
 Turnip your doorbell volume, I've been ringing it forever.

Knock, knock.
    Who's there?
    Carrot!
    Carrot who?
    Do you even carrot all?

Knock, knock.
    Who's there?
    Donut.
    Donut who?
    I donut know. You tell me.

FEATURED ARTWORK #2

*Knock, knock. Who's there? Sword. Sword who? Sword of easy to find out,
just open the door. (Artwork by Samuel Hennessy)*

3

A BUNCH OF DIFFERENT JOKES

Knock, knock.
  Who's there?
  Déjav.
  Déjav who?
  Knock, knock.

Knock, knock.
  Who's there?
  Island.
  Island who?
  Island on your roof by accident when I parachuted.

Knock, knock.
  Who's there?
  Aloha.
  Aloha who?
  Aloha myself down from your roof.

Knock, knock.
    Who's there?
    Hawaii.
    Hawaii who?
    I'm fine, how are you?

Knock, knock.
    Who's there?
    Amusing.
    Amusing who?
    Amusing your doorbell, but it doesn't work.

Knock, knock.
    Who's there?
    Avenue.
    Avenue who?
    Avenue heard the news? Open up.

Knock, knock.
    Who's there?
    Francis.
    Francis who?
    Francis is in Europe.

Knock, knock.
    Who's there?
    Europe.
    Europe who?
    Europe late.

Knock, knock.
> Who's there?
> Pasture.
> Pasture who?
> It's pasture bedtime, go to sleep.

Knock, knock.
> Who's there?
> Deluxe.
> Deluxe, who?
> Deluxe broken, I can't use my key.

Knock, knock.
> Who's there?
> Icy.
> Icy who?
> I see you haven't fixed your doorbell yet.

Knock, knock.
> Who's there?
> Juicy.
> Juicy who?
> Juicy this funny video on YouTube? It's hilarious.

Knock, knock.
> Who's there?
> Kenya.
> Kenya who?
> Kenya open the door, it's raining out here.

Knock, knock.
    Who's there?
    Alpaca.
    Alpaca who?
    Alpaca the suitcase, you load up the car.

Knock, knock.
    Who's there?
    Ash.
    Ash Who?
    I did not mean to make you sneeze.

Knock, knock.
    Who's there?
    Wiper.
    Wiper who?
    Wiper nose, it's running.

Knock, knock.
    Who's there?
    Tish.
    Tish who?
    Here you go, wipe your nose.

Knock, knock.
    Who's there?
    Moose.
    Moose who?
    Moose you be so nosy?

Knock, knock.
> Who's there?
> Cook.
> Cook who?
> I'm not crazy, you are.

Knock, knock.
> Who's there?
> Thermos.
> Thermos who?
> Thermos be a better knock knock joke than this.

Knock, knock.
> Who's there?
> Bach.
> Bach who?
> Bach, Bach, Bach, I'm a chicken.

Knock, knock.
> Who's there?
> Hammond.
> Hammond who?
> Hammond eggs for breakfast please.

Knock, knock.
> Who's there?
> Olive.
> Olive who?
> I love you, too.

Knock, knock.
    Who's there?
    Isma
    Isma who?
    Isma lunch ready yet.

Knock, knock.
    Who's there?
    Althea.
    Althea who?
    Althea later alligator.

Knock, knock.
    Who's there?
    Dimitri.
    Dimitri who?
    Dimitri is where hamburgers grow.

Knock, knock.
    Who's there?
    Adelia.
    Adelia who?
    Adelia the cards and we'll play Crazy Eights.

Knock, knock.
    Who's there?
    Dawn.
    Dawn who?
    Dawn leave me out here in the cold.

Knock, knock.
>Who's there?
>Anita.
>Anita who?
>Anita 'nother tissue.

Knock, knock.
>Who's there?
>Sore ewe.
>Sore ewe who?
>Sore ewe gonna open the door or not?

Knock, knock.
>Who's there?
>Aldo.
>Aldo who?
>Aldo it's raining, you can still come outside.

Knock, knock.
>Who's there?
>Amanda
>Amanda who?
>Amanda repair your doorbell.

Knock, knock.
>Who's there?
>Hello.
>Hello who?
>My name's not who.

Knock, knock.
    Who's there?
    Porpoise.
    Porpoise who?
    For all intents and porpoises the case is closed.

Knock, knock.
    Who's there?
    Chicken.
    Chicken who?
    Chicken to see how you are doing.

Knock, knock.
    Who's there?
    Guitar playing tuna.
    Guitar playing tuna who?
    Don't be silly, you can't tuna fish.

Knock, knock.
    Who's there?
    Door-bell repair man.
    Doorbell repair man who?
    No, seriously, I'm here to repair your doorbell.

Knock, knock.
    Who's there?
    Alfredo sauce.
    Alfredo sauce who?
    Alfredo sauce so many people waiting, he went home.

Knock, knock.
>Who's there?
Diesel.
Diesel who?
Diesel be a good day to go for a walk in the park.

Knock, knock.
>Who's there?
Dozen.
Dozen who?
Dozen anyone recognize my voice anymore?

Knock, knock.
>Who's there?
Knock knock.
Who's there?
No, you're supposed to say, "Knock knock, who?"

Knock, knock.
>Who's there?
Easily distracted pirate.
Easily distracted pirate who?
Arrr, look, a squirrel!

Knock, knock.
>Who's there?
Riot.
Riot, who?
Riot on time, you're here!

Knock, knock.
    Who's there?
    A boat.
    A boat, who?
    A boat time you answered the door.

Knock, knock.
    Who's there?
    Disguise.
    Disguise, who?
    Disguise de limit.

Knock, knock.
    Who's there?
    Sword.
    Sword, who?
    Sword of easy to find out, just open the door.

Knock, knock.
    Who's there?
    Wire.
    Wire, who?
    Wire you making me wait outside, let me in.

Knock, knock.
    Who's there?
    Waddle.
    Waddle who?
    Waddle we do for fun today?

Knock, knock.
　Who's there?
　Windy.
　Windy who?
　Windy you think you can come out to play?

Knock, knock.
　Who's there?
　Wooden shoe.
　Wooden shoe who?
　Wooden shoe like to know.

Knock, knock.
　Who's there?
　Yacht.
　Yacht who?
　Yacht to be happy, I'm here to visit

Knock, knock.
　Who's there?
　Your best friend.
　Your best friend who?
　Come on, you know your own best friend!

Knock, knock.
　Who's there?
　Impatient pirate.
　Impatient pirat-
　(Interrupting) Arrrrrrrh!

Knock, knock.
    Who's there?
    Deluxe.
    Deluxe, who?
    Deluxe Ness Monster.

Knock, knock.
    Who's there?
    Honey bee.
    Honey bee who?
    Honey bee a nice person and let me in.

Knock, knock.
    Who's there?
    A broken pencil.
    A broken pencil who?
    Forget it, there's no point.

Knock, knock.
    Who's there?
    Alaska.
    Alaska who?
    Alaska if you can come over to play.

Knock, knock.
    Who's there?
    Goat.
    Goat who?
    Goat side, it's sunny and warm.

Knock, knock.
> Who's there?
> Déjav.
> Déjav who?
> Knock, knock.

FEATURED ARTWORK #3

*Knock, knock. Who's there? A boat. A boat who? A boat time you
answered the door. (Artwork by Daniel Hennessy)*

4

YOUR FAVOURITE JOKE

What is your favourite knock knock joke that isn't in this book?

Send it to us at thehennessykids@gmail.com, and we'll look to share it online with all our friends.

ACKNOWLEDGMENTS

Special thank you to everybody who is getting our joke books out from their public library and then sharing jokes with their family and friends!

Thank you for reading our book! We hope you enjoyed it. Please tell these jokes to your friends and family and make more people happy.

ABOUT THE AUTHORS

The Hennessy Kids think the world would be better with more smiles.

Want to know when our new books and games are available? Sign up for our newsletter or visit www.hennessyent.com!

BOOKS BY THE HENNESSY KIDS

101 Funny Jokes, Vol. 1

101 Funny Jokes, Vol. 2

101 Pet Jokes

101 Knock Knock Jokes, Vol. 1

101 Knock Knock Jokes, Vol. 2

101 Knock Knock Jokes, Vol. 3

The Big Book Of Jokes

101 Nature Jokes

101 Food Jokes

101 Halloween Jokes

101 Christmas Jokes

101 School Jokes

Visit hennessyent.com for the complete up-to-date list of our books and games!

www.ingramcontent.com/pod-product-compliance
Lightning Source LLC
Chambersburg PA
CBHW070955120626
46546CB00004B/1619